Legacy of a
Miner's Daughter

The social changes of the
Banabans after phosphate mining

Stacey M. King

BANABAN VISION PUBLICATIONS

Gold Coast, Australia

Legacy of a Miner's Daughter: the impact on the Banabans after phosphate mining
Copyright © Stacey M. King.
All rights reserved.
Published by Banaban Vision Publications
PO Box 1116 Paradise Point. Qld. 4216. Australia
www.banabanvision.com

A catalogue record for this work is available from the National Library of Australia

NATIONAL
LIBRARY
OF AUSTRALIA

Isbns:
Paperback: 978-0-6451491-0-4
Ebook: 978-0-6451491-7-3

Cover designed by Stacey King

This content was written by the author and presented at:
ISLANDS of the WORLD VIII International Conference
"Changing Islands – Changing Worlds"
1-7 November 2004, Kinmen Island (Quemoy), Taiwan

The author has provided information sourced from original documents, photographs and interviews either owned or kindly donated to the author. All other reference material has been sourced as quoted. Internal diagrams were created and/or supplied by the author.

DEDICATION

Raobcia Ken Sigrah
1956-2021
Banaban Clan spokesman and historian

Your name will live on in history as a true Banaban warrior and a proud descendant of his people, who gave your people the greatest gift:

"Hold your head high and be forever proud of being BANABAN and ensure Banaban identity is never lost but passed on to future generations".

'If Ocean Island is what I think it is, there is a fortune in it, if not several.'

Albert Ellis on board s.s. Archer, 14th March 1900.

'As the friendly unsuspecting Banaban population numbering only 451 people welcomed Ellis to their shores, they had no conceivable idea that his arrival would herald the beginning of the end.'

Stacey King.

Contents

Photographs

1. Map showing phosphate deposits on Banaba – May 1904.

Introduction

On remote Banaba Island lies a tale of deep significance—
a tale of 80 years of phosphate mining and its far-reaching
consequences on the island's indigenous inhabitants, the
Banabans. Understanding the origins and discovery of
phosphatic rock is the key to unlocking the subsequent
transformation that shaped the lives of the Banabans and
gave rise to a Pacific phosphate industry with global impli-
cations in world trading markets.

Peering through the lens of history, we witness the birth
of an industry that forever altered the fate of the island and
its people. The once-pristine shores of Banaba became the
epicentre of an endeavour that promised prosperity but left
indelible marks on the cultural fabric of the Banabans. By
unearthing the layers of the past and shedding light on the
profound ramifications that unfolded over eight tumultu-
ous decades.

The Banabans struggles, and their unwavering resili-
ence in the face of adversity is a testament to the strength
of a community confronted with the harsh realities of the
human condition and their pursuit of justice and survival
against all odds.

More than four decades have passed since the cessation of phosphate mining on Banaba, and the Banaban community now face new challenges. This situation underscores the international community's responsibility to ensure the Banabans continued survival during the challenging years ahead.

2. The discovery of this phosphate rock would change the lives of the Banaban people forever.

European discovery

The discovery of phosphate rock in the Pacific by Albert Ellis from the Sydney office of the London-based Pacific Islands Phosphate Company (PPIC) and his subsequent arrival on Banaba Island on 28th August 1900 would signify the most significant turning point in Banaban history.

The global impact of Ellis's discovery of what had long been regarded as a piece of 'fossilised tree' used as the office doorstop would also provide a lifeline for PIPC, which was struggling financially to remain afloat.

As the friendly unsuspecting Banaban population numbering only 451 people welcomed Ellis to their shores, they had no conceivable idea that his arrival would herald the beginning of the end. The Banabans as a people had just become expendable.

The first recorded sighting of Banaba (Paanopa or Panapa according to Admiralty charts) was by Captain Jered Gardener on 3rd January 1801 aboard the American ship *Diana*. At first, he mistook Banaba for what he referred to as nearby Byron Island, and on realising his mistake, he named his new discovery Rodman's Island after the vessels' owners Rodman and Company of New Bedford.

STACEY M. KING

However, it was not until 1804 that Captain John Mertho, aboard his ship *Ocean* would claim the official discovery of the island and its English name – Ocean Island. This name would also signify the subsequent Colonial possession of Banaba Island until 1980.

Banaba Island, a small isolated outcrop consisting of 595 hectares, is situated in the Pacific; latitude 0.52 south and longitude 169.35 east, just 83 kilometres south of the Equator and 180 kilometres from its nearest neighbour Nauru. The island lies in the full rush of the equatorial current running at a varying strength between 2 to 5 kilometres per hour.

Roughly round in shape except for a bay, approximately 1.2 kilometres in length, situated on the island's southern side, offering a natural landing place for small boats and canoes. The diameter of the island, north and south, east and west, is virtually the same, measuring approximately 2.5 kilometres and reaching over 85 meters at its highest point.

In fact, Banaba forms the almost circular top of a steep and very symmetrical submarine mountain that, over the millennia, has been submerged numerous times, resulting in a composition of coral, with phosphate on top from the highest points to depths in some areas of up to 18 metres. (Figure 1.1).

Pacific Fertilizer Industry

In 1871 the world's fertiliser industry was transformed when Agricultural chemists discovered the significance of phosphorus in the ecological system and the value of soluble phosphate in unlocking plant nutrients lying virtually dormant in the soil. This discovery heralded the beginning of a new fertiliser industry based on phosphate rock treated with sulphuric acid.

During this period, large deposits of rock and alluvial phosphate had been discovered on the American continent and in Morocco and Tunisia, which were expected to meet the needs of American and European farmers for a least the next century. While Australian and New Zealand farmers depended on regional phosphatic guano deposits (accumulation of bird droppings).

However, guano was limited in content and quality and scattered across the vast breadth of the Pacific Ocean from the west coast of America to the northeast peak of Australia. These guano deposits had been methodically worked with 'broom-shovel-and-wheelbarrow-technology', offering a very limited and frugal future (Williams & Macdonald 1985:7).

By 1899 the teams working in the Western Pacific were scraping up residual loads of guano assaying as low as 30 percent phosphate of lime, while farmers were demanding 60 percent.

Ellis's discovery in 1900 would provide both the lifeline for the ailing PPIC and a financial windfall far beyond the company's expectations, while Australian and New Zealand farming interests would also reap the benefits of increased production yields that had never been previously envisaged.

The remote and previously insignificant Banaba Island, now officially 'discovered' as Ocean Island, had just become a very valuable and sought-after asset.

The island's indigenous inhabitants were all that remained in the way of this timely discovery. Up until this period of Pacific history, Ocean Island had been considered by European seamen as 'a curiously dry and uninviting place seldom visited except by occasional missionary or trader' (Williams & Macdonald 1985:14) and known to be beyond the limits of German jurisdiction north of the Equator.

It was considered so insignificant and isolated that in 1892 the British Government did not bother including the island in their newly formed Gilbert and Ellice Colony Protectorate. Even with Ellis's discovery, the British Government still needed to be convinced, as reported by the Western Pacific High Commissioner, Sir George O'Brien. In a telegram from his Suva office dated 9th

February 1900, after receiving a report on the situation by the Gilbert and Ellice Island Colony (GEIC) High Commissioner, W. Telfer Campbell, the previous day, he stated:

2. As Ocean Island is said to possess no harbour, and to be difficult of access owing to the prevalence of very strong currents, there would appear to be no reason for including it in the Gilbert & Ellice Protectorate merely for the purpose of preventing its falling into the hands of some other Power. And as Mr. Campbell points out, its inclusion would add to the expenditure of the Protectorate without bringing in any adequate compensating revenue. This being so it would seem that the only ground would seem that the only ground for adding the island to the Gilbert & Ellice Protectorate is in order to facilitate the acquisition by the Pacific Islands Company or rights over the guano which it is supposed to contain, and I fail to see why the Company should not be left to make such arrangements in that respect as may be satisfactory to both parties.

3. ... I can ascertain no application has ever been made by the inhabitants of the island for British protection, and it is possible that they might resist Mr. Campbell if he were to proclaim it as included in the Gilbert & Ellice Protectorate. ... If decided on, it would I think, be well that the proclamation should be made on the visit of some man of war to the island.

4. I am unable to understand the application by the Company as for a Guano licence, as such licences are issued only in the case of uninhabited and unclaimed island, or reefs. Possibly the Company was under the impression that Ocean Island is uninhabited, but I am informed that it is rather thickly inhabited.

5. I may add that the passage in your telegram, "and then proceed as proposed in the case of Solomons grants" would seem to require some explanation in the event of your directing me to proceed in the matter. The proposed Solomons grants are grants by the High Commissioner of waste lands, and the rents of such lands as may be leased will go to the revenue of the Solomons Protectorate; while the Guano on Ocean island is private property at the disposal of the owners who, if they part with it, will be entitled to the consideration paid for it.

The Solomon Project, referred to by O'Brien, was a visionary scheme based on the hope that the Pacific Islands Company (PIC) would be given a ninety-nine-year lease on 200,000 acres (80,937 hectares) to be developed as a comprehensive plantation-based settlement in the achievement of which objective the natives would be gradually brought from a condition of squalid and brutal heathenism to a state of Christian decency. At the same time, British trade and commerce would be increased. (Williams & Macdonald 1985:15)

8

The negotiations begin

With these latest developments, Ellis proceeded to Banaba, arriving aboard the *Archer* at dawn on 3rd May 1900, where Banaban canoes quickly paddled out to greet the ship. Among this group, Ellis would wrongly surmise that one of the men who came aboard to welcome him must be the island's chief and, therefore, 'King' of the entire Island community.

On the same day as his arrival and with major assumptions, not to mention that there was no mutually understandable language between the parties, Ellis had the Banabans put crudely formed 'crosses' on a quickly drawn-up document. An 'Agreement'. that would grant the Pacific Islands Company Limited the rights to mine phosphate for the rate of £50 per annum for the next 999 years.

This document would become known and branded as scandalous throughout the years that would follow. In later years, Ellis himself, in his various writings, would admit that he soon discovered that there was no one 'Chief' or 'King' on Banaba at all. He quickly redrafted his famous document to accommodate so-called 'Chiefs' from the island's four villages and include their thumbprints to try and legitimise his original 'Agreement'. In fact, Temati, the Banaban man he had wrongly accredited as the 'King' of the Banabans, was the man, under Banaban cultural protocols, with the inherited duty to board foreign vessels when they arrived.

3. Albert Ellis' camp at Tabwewa, Ocean Island (Banaba) 1900.

It is hard to know whether Ellis's mistake was genuine on his part or more the need to speed up and formalise his company's possession of the island's phosphate deposits, especially given the attitude of the British Government. However, what is known is from this point in history, Ellis and his company's continued dealings with the Banabans and the misinterpretation of Banaban culture and traditions would leave a tragic and lasting legacy that still persists to this day.

At this stage, a new and proclaimed official European version of Banaban history was created and began to advance at a pace to rival the ever-evolving phosphate industry. With only 451 Banabans standing in the way of progress, the essence of their identity as Banabans had now become dispensable. Before the unsuspecting Banaban landowners knew, Ellis had negotiated and documented purchases of their land and leases in the Banaban village of Tabwewa and Uma.

By September 1900, he had organised the building of an island jetty and a storehouse to house foodstuffs and perishable goods while his men had taken up residence in tents or under tarpaulins.

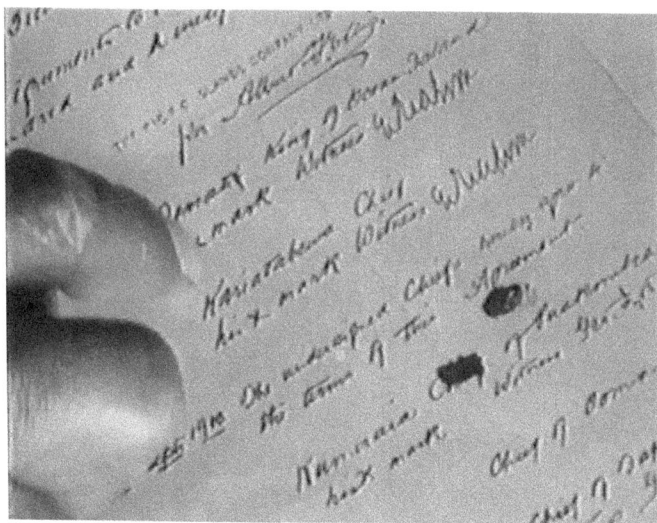

4. Banaban Elders signatories on Ellis' original contract Ocean Island (Banaba), in 1900.

5. Albert Ellis mistakes Banaban elder Temate as the 'King' of Ocean Island (2nd front right with waistcoat).

The struggle for land and the consequences for the Banabans

Ellis and his Company soon discovered that the Banabans would not work for them. While the Banabans initial 'welcome' soon began to sour when they saw their land and valuable food trees disappearing before their eyes. Their initial eagerness to place their marks on documents or carry and pick up rocks for their new visitors had disappeared.

As Ellis stated in his diary during his initial negotiations with the Banabans to acquire the land he needed to commence mining:

> The men said they only had small pieces and the coconut trees thereon meant their livelihood, therefore they could not sell – but that we were at liberty to build houses, shipping places, lay tram lines or do nay work on their land, provided the coconuts and gardens were not interfered with. (Williams & Macdonald 1985:34)

This entry and other significant negotiations made during his initial visit, in what Ellis referred to as being not difficult to clinch, reflect the attitude and intentions of Ellice and the PPIC towards the Banabans from the beginning. He was worried the Banabans would begin to 'get and exalted view of the value of their deposits' as prospecting progressed (Williams & Macdonald 1985:33).

Other important aspects of these first negotiations included payments to the Banabans made in chits for trade or Letters of Credit back to the PPIC. Ellis also recommended that no other white men, apart from those who worked for his company, should be allowed to live on the island, which was agreed to.

This significant step by Ellis would give his company virtually total control over the island now and in the future. The Company had also convinced the British Government to annex Banaba (Ocean Island) into their Gilbert and Ellice Island Protectorate six months later, on 28th November 1900. By the end of 1900, the Company had already shipped 1550 tons of phosphate from the island.

The Banabans were now on an erroneous path of sequential events that they had no understanding or concept of the magnitude of what their kind 'welcoming' gesture would perpetuate. The following episodes are part of that process that would escalate over the next century leaving the Banabans in the precarious position they are in today.

By 1902 the Pacific Phosphate Company Limited (PPC) was registered as a subsidiary of the PPIC, and the

Banabans leases and licenses were transferred. This new company also included some influential International businessmen, including German financial interests, with Germans, allowed to sit on the board with the other British directors (Sigrah & King 2001:223).

By 1909 life as far as the Company was concerned had become civilised and generally pleasant. In addition to between 400 and 500 Banabans, the status-graded population now consisted of around 1,000 recruited Pacific Island labourers (mainly from the nearby Gilbert & Ellice Island Group), 400 or more Japanese, and some 80 European company staff, together with a small contingent of Fijian police (Williams & Macdonald 1985:84).

What also should be noted at this stage of development was that Banaba had now become a fully industrialised Island with electrical lighting, machinery, and operating facilities that would prove to be the leading-edge technology of the time. By this period, the relationship between the Company and the Banabans had further deteriorated to the stage that the Banabans were refusing to lease or sell any more of their land.

Up until 1913, all Banaban land acquired by the Company for phosphate mining had to be negotiated with individual Banaban landowners under so-called Phosphate and Tree Purchase deeds for a fixed sum averaging around £20 an acre, which, together with the payment of £50 a year under the Agreement and compensation for the loss of any food-producing trees, was the sole payment given to the Banabans (Maude 1946:4).

This stalemate would continue until 1913, when the Government and Company finally brokered another agreement with the Banaban landowners to sell off another 145 acres (58.6 hectares) of their valuable land.

By the time of the 1913 Land Agreement, the Banabans argued that they should receive 'compensation for food-producing trees destroyed as under the previous Phosphate and Tree Purchase deeds' (Maude 1946:4). They also believed the phosphate company had made inaccurate records of land features and measurements, and approximate measurements were not longer acceptable to them (Sigrah & King 2001:224).

The Banabans were also starting to make other objections, accusing the company of switching leases from outside to inside of mining boundaries. They also were concerned that the replanting of food-bearing trees was impracticable, especially during times of drought. The issue over land boundaries would not be addressed until 1931 when Maude was appointed by the Colonial Government as Native Lands Commissioner. However, thirty-one years of illegal acquisition of Banaban lands by the mining company would go unchecked by this time.

The next major event to befall the island was World War One. Because the island was already under British government administration, minimal impact was felt on Banaba except for thirty-five Company staff that returned to Australia and New Zealand to enlist.

Meanwhile, the situation at the Company's sister mining operations on Nauru, which were under German governance and administration, now found themselves as the enemy. The Germans had placed the island's British staff under house arrest. This situation was resolved three months after the start of the war when the S.S. *Messina* took Nauru's German workforce for interment back in Australia.

Even though the Banabans were under constant conflict with the Company, they genuinely believed in the 'Good King George' as they affectionately referred to the King of England. On hearing that the Good King was under attack by Germany, the Banabans gave a gift of 1,000 pounds to the Prince of Wales Relief Fund.

With the end of World War One, another significant development was about to unfold.

6. Resident Commissioner EC Elliot (centre right) and Arthur Grimble (centre left) with Ocean Island mining staff enlistees and Police band during WWI.

The governments of United Kingdom, Australia and New Zealand take over

As the war drew to a close, the Australian Prime Minister of Australia, William Hughes, was in London to discuss postwar problems directly affecting Australia, including the Allies retention of German possessions in the Pacific.

By February 1919, the delegation to the Peace-making Council of Ten met to discuss what was wanted by the group in the way of mandates.

The discussions started with a proposal that New Zealand should have Western Samoa, Nauru should be brought within the jurisdiction of the Western Pacific High Commission, and German New Guinea should go to Australia, and the islands above the Equator to Japan (Williams & Macdonald 1985:126).

With Hughes' insistence, it was later decided that Nauru should also be included in the Australian allocation. Nauru would be the catalyst for the Dominion Prime Ministers of Australia and New Zealand to flex their muscles with each other, the British Government, and the mining company. During these negotiations, Hughes was adamant that Nauru should come under the total control of Australia. However, on 27th June 1919, a compromise was finally reached where the three governments of Australia, New Zealand and the United Kingdom would share the Mandate over Nauru.

7. View of an Industrialised Banaba early 1900s.

This ensuing Mandate also meant the acquisition of the Phosphate Company's rights and assets over mining on Nauru. The only thing left was to decide how much to pay for the total operation. On 18th February 1920, the privately owned PIC was brought out by the three governments of the United Kingdom, Australia and New Zealand conjointly for the sum of £3.5 million. It was renamed the British Phosphate Commission (BPC).

This created another dilemma as it became apparent that running Ocean Island in competition with Nauru would be absolutely fatal to the new Company in every way. With this in mind and the fact that Nauru would be run as a non-profit enterprise by the three governments involved,

Banaba was also officially included in the deal by June of the same year.

This complex and protracted agreement would be called the Nauru Agreement of 1919, and under Article 14 of the Agreement, the following allocation and contributions were to be made:

> Each of the three Governments shall be entitled to an allotment of the following proportions of the phosphate produced or estimated to be produced in each year, namely:
> - United Kingdom: 42%
> - Australia: 42%
> - New Zealand: 16%
>
> Provided that such allotment shall be for home consumption for agricultural purposes in the country of allotment, and not for export (Williams & Macdonald 1985:135).

In a 1919 report tabled in the New Zealand Parliament titled – *Nauru and Other Phosphate Islands in the Pacific,* it was claimed that Banaba 'contains 15 million tons of phosphate of tolerably uniform quality, and corresponding on the dry substance to 85.25 to 86.75 percent of tricalcic phosphate. As in the case of Nauru, the greater part goes to Australia and Japan'.

It was soon apparent that Article 14 of the Agreement would cause much consternation between the three governments.

By 1924 when 1.5 million tons had been shipped, 950,000 tons had gone to Australia, 160,000 to New Zealand, and only 30,000 tons to Britain, while 36,000 tons had gone to Japan and other countries. The distribution system was developing efficiently, and sales in Australasia were expected to reach more than £1 million a year by 1925.

8. The devastating impact of phosphate mining on Banaba by 1920.

However, during this period, the young Banaban men were making it very clear that they had no intentions of making any more land available to the newly formed BPC. This situation would escalate in 1927 when the land previously acquired under the 1913 Agreement was nearly depleted.

The BPC negotiations with the Banaban landowners had ground to a halt with what the Commissioners considered unreasonable demands by the Banabans. The Banabans refusal would cost them dearly as the Island's Resident Commissioner Arthur Grimble stepped into the fray, punishing them by forbidding games and establishing a curfew from 6pm to 6am. Yet, the Banabans still refused the BPC terms (Binder 1977:83).

Grimble, at his wit's end, then took extreme measures by writing to the Banabans, threatening actual violence if they did not accept the BPC terms.

This written document would emerge in its entirety fifty years later during the Banabans court proceeding against the BPC, bringing Grimble's actions finally to account. It was also during this period that a telegram was dispatched on 22nd October 1927 by His Excellency the Governor-General of Australia on behalf of the Prime Minister to the Secretary of State for Dominion Affairs stating clearly their intentions regarding the Banaban issue. The following from Prime Minister begins: –

The term offered by the Commissioners are in excess of those recently agreed at Nauru and amply cover the differences in conditions between that Island and Ocean Island providing both for the present and future welfare of the Banabans. As all the phosphate on Ocean Island will eventually be required it appears to Commissioners advisable that steps should be taken to secure another island or islands for the use of the

Banabans when Ocean Island is no longer suitable for their habitation, and the Commissioners have expressed their willingness to co-operate in their matter. The question of immediate removal to another island can be avoided if the land now required is made available without restrictive terms and conditions ... Commissioners, therefore, request:

a) that phosphate mining land at Ocean Island be made available without delay for use as required by the British Phosphate Commissioners upon terms not exceeding those agreed at Ocean Island early in July and approved by the commissioners and the Colonial Office;

b) terms and conditions for leasing land at Ocean Island for purposes other than phosphate mining be arranged for 20 years on the same basis as at Nauru;

c) that it be recognised that the whole deposit of phosphate at Ocean Island must eventually be worked;

d) that arrangement be made for the acquisition of another island or islands suitable for eventual occupation by the Banabans.

As you have doubtless been advised in similar terms by United Kingdom Commissioner shall be glad to hear your views. My Government concurs generally with the recommendation but considers the suggested transfer of Banabans to another island raises somewhat serious issues. We do not consider we are justified in making such a recommendation as this matter is one entirely within the province of British Administration.'(Sigrah & King 2001:323-324)

By the end of the year, the United Kingdom was ready to consider legislation for the compulsory acquisition of Banaban land on the grounds that the phosphate under the surface belonged to the Crown.

This was an absolute negation of the Phosphate and Trees Agreement 1903, which was based on the premise that the Banabans owned not only whatever grew on the surface but also the underlying phosphate deposits.

It was also a complete reversal of Colonial Office policy as expressed in 1923 by the then Secretary of State for the Colonies, who had stated plainly that the rights of Banabans extended to full ownership of their land and the 'minerals there under' (Williams & Macdonald 1985:227).

9. Arthur Grimble, Resident Commissioner, had the role of enforcing Compulsory Land Acquisition.

The 1928 Compulsory Land Acquisition

It was during this struggle that the Government took what Maude would eloquently describe years later while writing his Memorandum on the Future of the Banabans, as '...the Government had perforce to intervene, with the acquisition of land on Ocean island.' (Maude 1946:5)

In his role as the Government land surveyor, Maude had already been approached by the Banabans when they personally handed him a bag of gold with instructions to be so kind as to find and pay for a good lawyer to help them.

Reluctant to get in between the BPC and his superiors, Maude quickly handed over the bag to Resident Commissioner Grimble and promptly told him to return it to them post haste. In reality, the September Ordinance No. 4 of 1928 was enacted, giving the Resident Commissioner authority to enter into possession '... of any land required for mining if its owners refused to make it available under lawful and reasonable terms' (William & Macdonald 1985: 230).

By 1930 the Government had compulsorily taken over and leased an area of 150 acres (60.7 hectares) to the BPC for mining and another 27 ¾ acres (11.2 hectares) for more building and machinery installations. For the Banabans, their actions or protest now became unlawful as they tried to stand in the way of the Company mining any more land. Yet even with this in mind, the Banabans refused to give in, and as mining began, women clung to their precious food tress so that the bulldozer would have to destroy them too.

The area under acquisition was Buakonikai, the most fertile area on the island's central plateau. Here the Banabans food trees grew in abundance. Colony prisoners consisting mainly of nearby Gilbert Islanders were given a new role as acting policemen and, under instructions by Grimble, tore the helpless women from their trees. Even the Banabans' attempts to approach representatives of the BPC were met with armed constables (Binder 1977:83).

The Banabans now began a campaign of letter writing to the Secretary of State in London in an effort to tell the good King George what the BPC was doing to them. All this would fall on deaf ears. What is significant during this period is the actual intervention of the Government and the conflict of interests it surely represents.

The loose terminology used to describe the BPC as the Company is apparent in the study and dissection of historical data and material relating to phosphate mining on Banaba. It is important to remember that the Company was the British Phosphate Commission, a consortium owned and administered by the three powerful governments of the United Kingdom, Australia and New Zealand. This so-called, Company had the power and backing behind it to have laws written and enacted as it saw fit for the financial and political benefit of each country involved. The realisation that this presumably civilised Government authority supposedly on the island to protect them was now threatening to shoot them became a rude awaking to the Banabans on that fateful day in 1930.

Meanwhile, the Company recorded that phosphate shipped from their two island possessions of Banaba and Nauru had '...risen from almost 365 0000 tons to 575 000, which was being put into ships at half the f.o.b. price... Over a million tons of processed fertilisers were being distributed by the manufacturers at an approximate cost per ton of £5 in Australia and between £4 10s and £5 10s in New Zealand...' (Williams & Macdonald 1985:239).

But by 1930, other global events were in progress. Australia and New Zealand were now in the grip of a depression. The BPC used this period over the next few years to restructure and improve their operations. The depression had minimal impact on the lifestyle of the European Company staff living on Banaba, and in many cases, staff were finding their working conditions on the island a welcome relief from the poverty being experienced back home.

10. Banaban women tied themselves to their food trees to try and prevent mining.

Japanese invasion and the purchase of Rabi Island

By December 1940, the presence of German raiders in the Pacific was beginning to take its toll, especially when the Company's two prized vessels, the *Triadic* and *Triaster,* were sunk off Nauru.

By January 1941, the effects of the sinking of the ships and the shelling of Nauru would see a reduction in Banaba's shipping estimates. Even with mining operations working around the clock, the total shortfall in supplies to Australia and New Zealand would be 450 000 tons (Williams & Macdonald 1985:304).

Another interesting development was going on behind the scene, with the Commissioners feeling the pressure over reduced shipping rates being placed on them to stop supplying Japan until they were in a position to fully meet the demand of the partner countries. It was also surprising to see the British view of this situation at the time as being somewhat detached, as Colonial Office officials noted:

Australian and New Zealand politicians and businessmen were prone to show 'an undue nervousness of the activities and capabilities of Japan in the Pacific,' and in pressing for the evacuation of European women and children from the phosphate islands, they seemed to be inspired by 'humanitarian rather than military considerations' (Williams & Macdonald 1985:308).

While the BPC and Colonial Office were at odds and war was looming, a fund known as the Banaban Provident Fund was set up in 1931 to buy the Banabans a new home.

By 1940 the Government was actively searching for a suitable new island to accommodate them. But by 7th December 1941, the BPC faced other problems as the Japanese attacked the US naval base in Hawaii.

The BPC manager instructed staff to destroy the Company's equipment three days later. By dawn, the next day, the island's jetties, mooring buoys, span chains, launches, boats and company records had all been destroyed (Sigrah & King 2001:242).

By the beginning of 1942, American intelligence predicted that the Japanese were about to push southward into the Pacific. It was decided to evacuate the BPC staff on Banaba aboard the French destroyer *Le Triomphant* which arrived on Banaba on 28th February.

As the *Le Triomphant* set sail only hours later with 232 BPC staff and 823 Chinese labourers aboard, the acting Resident Commissioner Ron Third, and Lindsay Cole, the BPC labour inspector who was in charge of the 713 I-Kiribati and Tuvaluan workers and their families, decided to

remain behind. The workers and the local Banaban population had no choice but to stay, and with very limited food
rations left behind by the BPC, they returned to their food
trees and the sea to provide for their daily needs.

Not long after the evacuation from Banaba and the
abandonment of phosphate mining, the Banabans were
probably unaware of the official freehold purchase of Rabi
Island in Fiji that had been made on their behalf from their
own Provident funds for A£25,000.

For the Banabans, their first taste of freedom would only
last eight months when the Japanese landed in the August
of the same year. Life again on Banaba was about to change
with the arrival of a garrison of 500 Japanese troops and 50
labourers. While these new invaders quickly went about
fortifying the island and murdering and starving to death
many of the Banabans, I-Kiribati and Tuvaluan workers,
the BPC was already planning for the future rehabilitation
of Banaban and Nauru.

By December 1942 had issued the following statement,
'... Chief Engineer Thompson was drafting a comprehensive report on headway being made for the rehabilitation
of the islands, with plans in detail already on the drawing
board' (Williams & Macdonald 1985:323).

Staff from a Japanese company, Nanyo Kohatu Ka-
bushiki Kaisa, had been sent to Banaba to get the island
power plants and mining operations up and running again.
But their efforts were in vain because of the extent of BPC
sabotage. By 1943, a year after the invasion and with acute

food shortages, the Japanese removed all but 143 men from the island, sending the Banabans off to work in labour camps in Kosrae, Tarawa and Nauru.

By the end of the war, a total of 87 people, including I-Kiribati and Tuvaluan workers, had died from hunger or malnutrition, seven had perished at sea trying to escape the Japanese, three were beheaded, and 142 men were killed two days after the war was over. Banabans, I-Kiribati and Tuvaluan labourers had died or been murdered during the Japanese occupation. A total of 84 died by other means while 82 suffered injuries, including beatings, breaking of backs and limbs, stabbing by bayonet, and two reported cases of rape. A total of 349 people died on Banaba during the Japanese occupation (Sigrah& King 2001:256-257).

11. *Le Triomphant* set sail from Ocean Island (Banaba) with 232 BPC staff and 823 Chinese labourers aboard.

Exile from the homeland

While Australian forces landed on Banaba on the 1st October 1945, Albert Ellis had arrived on the island to represent the British Phosphate Commissioners at the official Japanese surrender. Meanwhile the Banabans were brought together on Tarawa and where Maude was there to meet them. Ellis was keen to take advantage of the situation and was already lobby the Colonial Office in Suva:

> ...while there is obviously a great advantage in the Banabans being transferred direct to Rabi... the matter will require careful handling. This opinion was shared by the New High Commissioner, Sir Alexander Grantham, who noted in a memorandum, 'If we can persuade them not to go back to Ocean Island we shall be spared many headaches' (Williams & Macdonald 1985:338).

Under these conditions and after nearly three years of maltreatment at the hands of the Japanese, the Banabans were confronted with the news that their villages and food trees had all been destroyed by the Japanese and that it would be impossible to reoccupy Banaba for at least two years.

They were completely unaware that while they were being told they would not be able to return to their homeland, the BPC had rehired company staff and, together with 49 I-Kiribati labourers, arrived on Banaba on 10th October 1945, only 10 days after the Japanese surrender of Banaba to Australia troops (Sigrah & King 2001:262).

The only real option afforded the Banabans was temporary resettlement on Rabi, where they would be given food rations for one month and housing, with a guarantee that they could return to their homeland after two years. If the Banabans refused the offer, they were told they would not be given any further financial assistance.

With the assistance of the BPC supplying one of their ships, the *SS Triona,* the Banabans were sent to Rabi, more than 3,200 km away in the Fiji Group. On 15th December 1945, 703 Banabans and 300 Gilbertese arrived on Rabi in the middle of cyclone season with army tents to provide shelter and enough food rations to sustain them for two months.

It was under these extreme and challenging conditions that Banabans arrived on Rabi, where they had difficulty trying to settle in and adjust to their new island. Over the years that followed, the Banabans became increasingly disillusioned. The level of discontent grew rapidly.

By June 1946, a joint Fiji – High Commission mission was sent to Rabi to investigate reports that the Banaban community was 'approaching sedition against the High Commissioner' (Maude 1946:15)

A report of their complaints was gathered, which included uncertainty over land rights on Ocean Island and Rabi. Also, their loss of confidence in Major Kennedy, the Island manager provided by the Government, increased incidences of sickness, particularly pulmonary troubles, diarrhea and measles, with the Banabans complaining they were having trouble with the damper climate.

This was particularly the case with the elderly, resulting in 27 deaths. Also, the inadequacy of housing facilities, which they believed was aggravating sickness. A third of the community was still living in tents proving challenging to withstand the climate and possible cyclones.

The lack of food and the fact the Banabans were prohibited from visiting neighbouring Fijian communities did not help the situation.

While the Banabans struggled to adjust to life on Rabi, life on Banaba was a very different story.

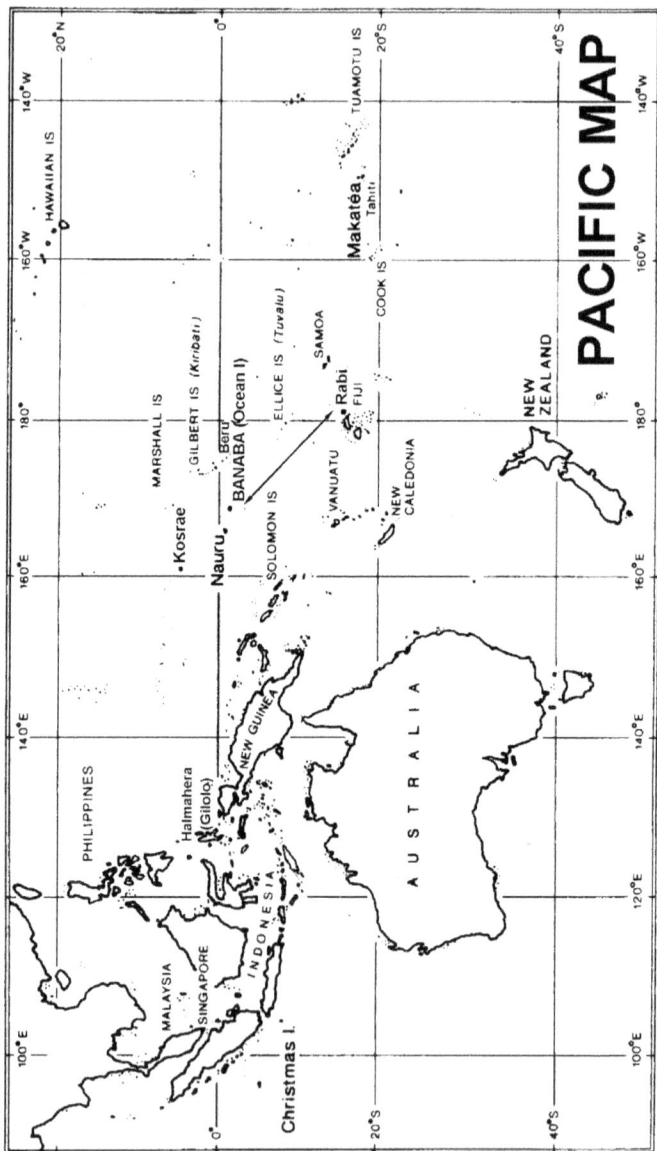

12. Banabans moved to Rabi Island, Fiji December 1945.

The UK Court Case

From this period, mining quickly resumed, with the Company now taking control of the island's mining operations and inhabitants. The one concession was that the Banabans had been granted permission to have a representative on the island to ensure that there would be no encroachment onto Banaban lands that were not part of the current lease agreements.

The representative's official role was to represent and protect the interests of the Banaban Landowners who had been moved to Rabi. It proved a difficult position as this lone Banaban liaised with the BPC and Colonial Office, which had all the backing and strength of the governments behind them.

Over this postwar period from 1945 to 1979, five Banaban men undertook this important role; their names are listed in order of their engagements:

1: Kabanti
2. Kaiekieki
3. Abitiai
4. Taungea
5. Kirite

13. Kaiekieki - Second Banaban Representative taken during his time on Banaba.

By 1965 the Banabans had come to the realisation that the British Government had no intentions of looking after their affairs. Frustrated by decades of constant disputes over their land leases back on Banaba and the inadequate royalties they were receiving from the BPC, they believed they had no choice but to instigate legal proceedings.

By January 1974, the Banabans extended their fight for justice by lodging a petition to the British Government for the legal separation of Ocean Island (Banaba) from Gilbert and Ellice Island Colony. This quest for independence would fall on 'deaf ears' as the British once again washed their hands of the Banaban issue and handed over responsibility to the newly formed Council of Ministers.

They would conclude that they considered Ocean Island 'an integral part of the Gilbert Islands, and added that it would oppose separation and independence for Ocean Island, either now or in the future' (Sigrah & King 2001:18).

United Kingdom
Banabans Seeking Justice

14. Banabans take their fight for justice to the UK High Court.

15. Banabans set up a camp behind the previous site of Uma village known as Tabonwaba, meaning 'Island Point'.

Banabans arrive to take control of their island

By 1977 while the Banabans took their case to an international level, the Banaban Elders on Rabi decided to send 100 young men from Rabi to the homeland to regain the island with the aim of halting mining by the BPC. The arrival of the Banaban contingent on the island had forced the Company and government's hand by insisting that their group be given permission to land.

Until this period, any Banabans trying to visit their homeland had to have written approval from the Colonial Office. After reluctantly being given permission to land and receiving a 'cool reception' by the Company officials and staff who had been told by management 'not to mix with these Banaban troublemakers' (Lennon 1992), the Banabans began to set up a camp behind the previous site of Uma village on the south-east coast in an area known as Tabonwaba, meaning 'Island Point'.

Tensions on the island grew as the BPC and Colonial office brought in more I-Kiribati (Gilbertese) to act as local Island police and build up the police presence on the island ensuring that the troublesome Banabans would be kept under control. During this period, the Company also doubled their production levels on the island while its lawyers countered the Banaban's legal actions in London.

By 1979, with court proceedings still underway, another contingent was sent from Rabi to reinforce the Banaban numbers on the homeland. The mood of the Banabans by this stage had become more defiant and radical in terms of their usually well-mannered and gentle nature.

Elders back on Rabi made a monumental decision to send this new contingent consisting of young Banabans prepared men and women to 'die for the cause' (Sigrah & King 2001:19) if necessary and try and put a stop to the mining, at least until the British court had finished hearing their case and handed down a ruling.

As tensions grew, these young Banabans began to be arrested and beaten during various skirmishes and found themselves thrown into the island's jail. This tension and the fatal injury of one of their young men had only fueled the Banabans more as they planned a protest march targeted at the Company management to stop mining.

Only hours before the planned action, word came from Tuvaluan (Ellice) labourers employed by the BPC that the I-Kiribati police had been issued side-arms and had been given orders to 'shoot to kill'. It was only after Elders on Rabi received this news, and after much consideration, they issued instructions for their people to 'stand down' (Teai 1997). The thought of their beloved homeland being turned into a killing ground for their young generation was abhorrent to them.

From that moment, they focused on the legal proceedings still underway in London and also took up another major challenge that would see them knocking on the doors of the United Nations in an effort to seek separation from the British and their Gilbert & Ellice Island Colony (GEIC). The British planned to dissolve the GEIC and return sovereignty to the people under the two new Island nations of Kiribati for the formerly Gilbert Island group and Tuvalu for the Ellice group.

All these cumulative actions drew to an end, and after 221 days and 10,000 documents that had been examined in the British High Court case, the judge finally handed down his verdict on the Banaban case. He found that the BPC had;

> ...failed to keep their promise to replant the Banabans land. The Banabans should get damages but just how much he could not bring himself to say. This they must go away to settle with the British Phosphate Commission. For the failure to restore the ravaged land he said:
>
> "The damages shall not be token not minimal but not large."
>
> He discounted the argument that nowadays mined land must legally be restored. However potent such arguments may be in political or social fields, they cannot affect the law of contract.

The second case on the breach of trust issue was finely balanced and could clearly have gone either way. Judge McGarry eventually decided the British Government was not, in fact, trustees for the Banabans. The British were therefore not technically liable for the injustices committed in their name and in the cause of immense millions of pounds' profit from phosphate.

...The judge concluded with most usual recommendation:

"I am powerless to give the plaintiff any relief, but in litigation against the Crown I think a judge must direct attention to a wrong that he cannot right and leave it to the Crown to do what it considers proper. The Crown is traditionally the fountain of justice and justice is not confined to what is enforceable in the court. The question is not whether the Banaban should succeed as a matter of fairness or ethics or morality. I have no jurisdiction to make an award just because I conclude they have a raw deal." (Binder 1977:165)

With the Court findings and public and parliamentary pressure, the BPC offered (provided the Banabans did not appeal in their action against the Crown) to set up a trust fund to produce a pension for the Banaban community (Sigrah & King 2001:19). It would take the Banabans another 4 years before they would accept the $AUD10 million offered.

The last shipment of phosphate leaves Banaba

At the same time, the BPC had been under increasing pressure from various lobby groups supporting the Banaban's cause, especially a BBC documentary that had gone to air in the United Kingdom. Finally, exposing the story to an unsuspecting public. With mounting public opinion building, the BPC's last phosphate shipment left Banaba's shores in November 1979.

As a final parting gesture and to show the Company's appreciation to the newly emerging Kiribati nation, they donated all removable fittings and equipment to the Kiribati government (Teai 1997). This action resulted in further tension between the Banabans and the Kiribati government, which they considered their new sovereign masters.

BPC had reportedly done the right and honourable thing with this gesture, but in fact, what it amounted to was the leaving of their mining machinery, plant and industrial debris behind on Banaba, saving them millions of dollars in rehabilitation or removal of asbestos-laden facilities for the Banabans to live amongst.

From the Island's original 595 hectares (1,500 acres), only 61 hectares (150 acres) would remain unmined. The BPC's final accelerated mining production proved very effective, as all that remained was mainly the ground under the buildings they had left behind.

Even along the island's roadways, mining encroached right to the edge of the bitumen. It was dangerous to wander away from these thoroughfares as the remaining razor-sharp coral pinnacles in some regions of the island reached 18 metres in depth.

16. Hospital theatre light, the only removable fitting left behind by the Kiribati government in 1979.

There was one final defiant gesture by the Banabans. After seeing the island's hospital completely stripped bare, except for the large operating light in the theatre, which had refused to budge, they began to damage various items. This included medical equipment, medicines, machinery etc., not wanting to hand it over to the Kiribati government, who planned to take the spoils away to other islands throughout the group.

It is important to realise that these actions undertaken by the Banabans and their negative outcomes were only due to the phosphate industry and the various 'turning points' or historical events chronicled in this study.

These episodes or sequences of erroneous events set into action the building of a regime that would entirely re-press and silence the Banaban people over the 80 year period it took to mine Banaba of its phosphate. It would undermine any efforts they made to try and decide their own future during the period and in the years that followed.

The BPC, under the auspices of the Colonial Government, had also deliberately built tension and rivalry between the Banabans nearby Island neighbours, the I-Kiribati, in an effort to use them to do their dirty work and remain aloof in their handling of the continual 'Banaban problem' has it had become known over time.

17. Banaba (Ocean Island) at the peak of phosphate mining in 1968. The island has been left decimated.

Ongoing legacies and role of the international community

Today more than four decades since the cessation of mining on Banaba, nothing has been done to rehabilitate the island. The Banabans live amongst the crumbling ruins left behind by the BPC, and the community's lack of water supply dur- ing persistent droughts is a major problem.

During a 1997 visit to Banaba, the population was around 500 people. Now today it has dropped to about 250-300. There is no regular shipping to the island, no airstrip built, and most food is imported except for what the is- lands' surrounding reefs and waters provide. When the rain falls, Banaba can produce green vegetables and crops. Today only a handful of food trees remain, not enough to sustain the Island's community as it did over the centuries.

The Banabans $10m Trust Fund was published in UNESCO's Banaban Report (Hindmarsh 2002) as expected to generate around F$360,000 that year with an operating budget of just F$5000,000, including add-ons of Fiji Gov- ernment grants and other generated income and business charges. It also reported that it was not a lot of money when the Banabans were expected to run two islands 2,400 km apart, with a cost of around F$14,000 per month to maintain public works for the Banabans currently resettled back on Banaba today.

18. The aftermath of phosphate mining has left Banaba destroyed with no rehabilitation has been carried out.

Over the past years, the financial and physical situation on both islands has deteriorated rapidly. With no rehabilitation on Banaba or development and much needed infrastructure on Rabi, the survival for the Banaban people is becoming increasingly difficult.

Even with experience in trying to organise various aid projects for both Banaban communities, it proves a challenging task as aid has to be channelled through the two governments involved, Fiji for Rabi based projects and Kiribati for those on Banaba. When approaches have been made in the past direct to the Australian Government, the community status of the Banabans proves to be a major hurdle, blocking any direct approach to the governments involved in the BPC and mining of Banaba.

These legacies have to be addressed, and other alternatives found that will finally bring about a level of closure for the Banabans and their future generations. As an Australian descendant of the Phosphateers, it is imperative to raise the question, 'when does the onus of responsibility end?'.

As candidly summarised by a serving Australian diplomat regarding the attitude of the Australian Government towards the Banaban's continued call for justice, he believed the issue was 'dead and buried' as far as the Government was concerned. He also confirmed that the Government wanted to keep the case 'closed' and was not keen on publicity on the issue. His frank and honest observations raise a very valid point that is also relevant to the other governments involved in the Pacific Phosphate mining industry.

The international community is also responsible for ensuring that the fundamental human rights the Banabans have been denied for the past century are finally afforded them.

19. Banabans are determined to preserve Banaban culture and identity now and in the future.

Conclusion and recommendations

At the current rate of neglect and attrition the Banabans are experiencing, the need for lobbying and building public awareness at an international level is critical and cannot be delayed. While the three governments concerned pride themselves on their human rights and democratic free societies, they must also be accountable for their past actions and present inactions that have adversely impacted the Banaban people.

If the logical equation and corporate consideration that 450 Banabans stood in the way of an emerging industry worth billions, therefore naturally making them expendable. Then surely, in the scale of such insurmountable odds, it is not unreasonable or unaffordable to at least repair the damage these governments caused.

The Government of Japan also has to be included in any further actions. Their onus of responsibility must also be considered, especially regarding the forced removal of the Banabans from their homeland during their wartime invasion and subsequent occupation. With a Banaban population currently around 6,000, this type of positive outcome is achievable and essential. Areas of address should include:

1. Investigate avenues for seeking compensation through the legal processes of the International courts.
2. International lobbying and media campaigns that could bring pressure to bear on the governments directly involved in the mining of Banaba.
3. Building networks with other International and Pacific bodies and organisations, e.g. Amnesty International, Fiji Human Rights Commission, Greenpeace, Commonwealth Committee of Fiji, Mineral Policy Institute, Aidwatch, Pacific Concerns Resource Centre, Citizens' Constitutional Forum, UN of Minority Peoples, International Movement Against Discrimination and Racism.
4. Building public awareness campaigns highlighting areas of general concern, e.g. human rights and environmental concerns.

With all these objectives in mind and to ensure the future survival of the Banabans, proper support and sustainable resource development on Rabi and Banaba is also an essential part of the equation. As the United Nations Sub-Commission on the Promotion and Protection of Human Rights focuses on the phenomenon of globalisation which they state 'has attracted more significant global attention than perhaps any other issue in recent memory', the Banabans must also use these platforms to evoke their calls for 'accountability', 'justice' and 'onus of responsibility' on a global level.

In this study, we have identified key players and issues that clearly show the creation of illegal acts and dealings being tuned into 'so called' legal laws under the mantle of government interventions and what has been defined as gross acts of 'conflicts of interest'. Besides all else, it is evident in this study that an original population of only 450 Banabans would never stand in the way of the discovery of phosphate on their island

Amazingly because this whole episode of history has been labelled as 'progress' and 'good business', it masks the actual fact that the Company's arrival and subsequent 'take over' of Banaba by what must be remembered was, in fact, the governments of United Kingdom, Australia and New Zealand is no less an aggressive act as was the Japanese invasion during WWII.

These are the facts that need to be published, and not the re-writing and sanitising of history to paint a picture that we want to hear.

20. Banaban Elders who were signatories on the original contract that would change the destiny of their people and island
forever

References

Binder, Pearl. *Treasure Islands – The trials of the Banabans.* London, 1997.

Hindmarsh, Gerard. One Minority People – *A Report on the Banabans*, Commissioned by UNESCO, Apia. November, 2002.

Lennon, Edna. Former wife of BPC employee 1950-1965. Interview conducted by Stacey King, 1992.

Maude, H.C. and H.E. *The Book of Banaba*. IPS, University of South Pacific Fiji, 1995

Maude, H.E. *Memorandum on The Future of the Banaban Population of Ocean Island; With Special Relations to their Lands and Funds.* Chief Lands Commissioner, Gilbert and Ellice Islands Colony, 1946.

O'Brien, Sir George. Telegram transcript from Office of the High Commissioner for the Western Pacific, Suva Fiji, to Colony Office London, February 1900.

Sigrah, Raobeia Ken Sigrah and King, Stacey M. *Te Rii ni Banaba: backbone of Banaba*, IPS, University of South Pacific Fiji, 2001 (1st edition) 2019 (2nd edition).

Report on - *Nauru and Other Phosphate Islands in the Pacific.* New Zealand House of Representatives, 1919.

Teai, Tomas. Banaban Magistrate at time of interview, Rabi, 1997.

Williams, Maslyn and Macdonald, Barrie. *The Phosphateers.* Melbourne University Press 1985.

About the Author

Stacey M. King is a historian, author, entrepreneur, and philanthropist. She has been an advocate for the indigenous Banaban people for many decades.

In 1989, she began researching her family's history for a historical novel based on their lives titled – *Nakaa's Awakening: Land of Matang* (Book One; 2000).

In 1997, she formed a personal and collaborative partnership with the late Ken Raobeia Sigrah, a Banaban Clan historian and spokesperson. Their first published work, *Te Rii Ni Banaba - backbone of Banaba* (2001; 2019), is a history book written from an indigenous perspective and endorsed by Banaban Clan elders.

With the establishment of Banaban Vision Publications, Stacey is converting much of their writings and research findings into digital publications. Since the passing of her beloved partner, Raobeia Ken Sigrah, she is determined to continue his legacy in preserving Banaban history for future generations.

Other Titles By The Author

Banaban History Non-Fiction Book
Te Rii ni Banaba. First Edition: IPS, Suva, Fiji. 2001, Second edition, Banaban Vision Publications, Gold Coast, Australia 2019.
Australia Banaba Relations: the price of shaping a nation, Banaban Vision, Gold Coast, March 2023.

History Non-Fiction Book – Chapter in Book
The Banaba-Ocean Island chronicles: private collections, indigenous record-keeping, fact and fiction. Chapter 17, *Hunting the collectors*. Cambridge Scholars, UK. February 2011.

Historical Fiction
Nakaa's Awakening, Land of Matang. Banaban Vision Publications, Gold Coast, Australia, May 2021 (Book 1; 4-book series. Blend of history, biography and fictional reconstruction)

Articles and Presentations

Australia Banaba Relations: the price of shaping a nation is now a call for recognition
Banaba-Ocean Island Chronicles: Private collections and indigenous record-keeping proving fact from fiction
Cultural Identity of Banabans
Legacy of a Miners Daughter and Assessment of the Social Changes of the Banabans after Phosphate Mining on Banaba
Essentially Being Banaban in Today's World: The role of Banaban Law, Te Rii Ni Banaba (Backbone of Banaba) in a Changing World

Banaban Social Media sites by Authors
Abara Banaba–Come Meet the Banabans: banaban.com
Banaban Vision: banabanvision.com
Banaban Voice Facebook:
facebook.com/groups/banabanvoice/
Banaban Vision Blog: banabanvoice.ning.com/
Banaban Vision: banabanvision.com
Banaban Media: vocalmedia.com

Connect with Us:
Banaban Vision Publications
PO Box 1116 Paradise Point Qld 4216 Australia
Stacey M. King – Author's Page: staceymking.com
Email: admin@banaban.com
Te Rii Ni Banaba -Facebook group:
https://www.facebook.com/groups/296299534653304/

Linkedin: Ken Sigrah:
https://www.linkedin.com/in/ken-sigrah-821b5975/
Linkedin: Stacey King:
https://www.linkedin.com/in/stacey-king-4ba68a76/